Cat Files

Tiger

WRITTEN BY
BETHANY LATHAM

KidHaven
PUBLISHING

Published in 2027 by
KidHaven Publishing, an Imprint of Greenhaven Publishing, LLC
2544 Clinton St., Buffalo, NY 14224

Written by: Bethany Latham
Edited by: Rebecca Phillips-Bartlett
Designed by: Ker Ker Lee

Cataloging-in-Publication Data
Names: Latham, Bethany.
Title: Tiger / Bethany Latham.
Description: Buffalo, NY : KidHaven Publishing, 2027. | Series: Cat files | Includes glossary and index.
Identifiers: ISBN 9781534569652 (pbk.) | ISBN 9781534569669 (library bound) | ISBN 9781534569676 (ebook)
Subjects: LCSH: Tiger--Juvenile literature.
Classification: LCC QL737.C23 L384 2027 | DDC 599.756--dc23

Printed in China

CPSIA compliance information: Batch #QS27KH: For further information contact Greenhaven Publishing LLC at 1-844-317-7404.

Please visit our website,
www.greenhavenpublishing.com.
For a free color catalog of all our high-quality books,
call toll free 1-844-317-7404
or fax 1-844-317-7405.

Find us on

Photo Credits – Images courtesy of Shutterstock.com, unless otherwise stated.

Cover & Recurring – apiguide, slowmotiongli, Hung Chung Chih, BMR Creation, graficriver_icons_logo, Vector Tradition. 2–3 – Wirestock Creators. 4–5 – Michal Ninger, Nick Dale Photo, Holly S Cannon, Marcel Brekelmans. 6–7 – Kathrine Andi, Michal Ninger. 8–9 – Danny Ye, Soumyajit Nandy, Ondrej Prosicky. 10–11 – Eric Isseleel. 12–13 – SMatrishva Vyas, Sourabh Bharti, TigerStocks. 14–15 – Sourabh Bharti, Atanu Chowdhury, Sourabh Bharti, Melanie Miedler. 16–17 – Michal Ninger, Sush4all. 18–19 – WilliamRoggero, SenecaS. 20–21 – Matjoe, Tomas Hejlek. 22–23 – Souradeep_ Chakraborty, Michal Ninger.

Contents

Words that look like <u>this</u> can be found in the glossary on page 24.

Big Cats

Big cats are powerful, meat-eating predators. Predators hunt the animals they eat. Scientists group big cats together because they have many things in common. This includes strong bodies, good eyesight, and sharp teeth.

Cheetah

Tiger

All cats belong to the Felidae family of animals. There are smaller groups within this family. The Pantherinae group includes big cats such as lions, tigers, and snow leopards. Another group is called Felinae. It includes cheetahs.

Snow leopard

Lion

FACT FILE

DIET:	Meat-eaters, or carnivores
ANIMAL TYPE:	Mammal
HUNTING:	Predator

Tigers

Tigers are the largest big cat. There are different types of tigers that live in different parts of Asia. Tigers can be found in 13 countries, including Russia and India.

Some types of tigers are the Bengal, Indochinese, South China, Siberian, Malayan, and Sumatran tigers.

FACT FILE

CONTINENT:	Asia
SIZE:	Up to 11 feet (3.5 m) long (without tail)
WEIGHT:	From 238 to 661 pounds (108 to 300 kg)
SPEED:	Up to 40 miles (65 km) per hour

Habitat

An animal's habitat is its natural home. Tigers live in many different habitats. These include rainforests, savannas, and pine forests. Tigers need lots of trees and plants to hide in.

Around half of all wild tigers live in India.

Some Bengal tigers live in mangrove swamps. These are coastal jungles. They are very wet with lots of trees.

Bengal tiger

Bengal tigers are the only coastal-living tigers.

Siberian tigers live in large, cold forests called taiga. There is usually a lot of snow there.

Siberian tiger

Body

Tigers have white spots on the backs of their ears.

Tigers all have some important body parts.

Tigers have rough tongues for licking meat off bones.

Tigers' teeth are very long and powerful.

Tigers have large, powerful front legs. Their back legs are longer than their front legs.

Tiger fur has a bold striped pattern.

Tigers' bodies are very strong and agile.

Tiger paws are large and powerful.

Tigers have sharp, retractable claws.

Blending In

The stripes on a tiger's fur help it camouflage itself. The stripes look like sunlight and shadows through trees. This makes the tiger harder to see. This camouflage is called concealing, fixed camouflage.

There is a tiger in this picture!

FACT FILE

COLOR:	Orange, black, and white
PATTERN:	Striped
FUR LENGTH:	Short
CAMOUFLAGE TYPE:	Concealing and fixed

Most humans can see the color orange. The animals tigers eat cannot. To them, orange and green look the same. This makes tigers even harder to spot.

Hunting Prey

Tigers only eat meat. They eat lots of different animals, including deer, pigs, cows, and goats. Tigers hunt at night. Sometimes, they travel up to 20 miles (32 km) in one night to find food.

Chital deer

Moupin pig

Tigers usually only eat one meal a week.

Tigers are ambush hunters. They sneak up on their prey from behind. Then, they pounce! They kill their prey by biting its neck.

FACT FILE

CLAW LENGTH:	Up to 4 inches (10 cm)
TEETH LENGTH:	Up to 3 inches (8 cm)
FOOD EATEN:	Up to 88 pounds (40 kg) in one night

Family Life

Tigers are usually solitary animals. This means they live alone. Young tigers are called cubs. Mothers and cubs stay together while the cubs are growing. This small group is called a streak of tigers.

A group of adult tigers is called an ambush.

Each tiger has its own territory. They show other tigers where their territory is using urine and claw marks and by rubbing their cheeks on trees. This is called scent marking.

FACT FILE

GROUP NAME:	Streak or ambush
GROUP SIZE:	Up to five
COMMUNICATION:	Scent marking

Raising Young

A mother tiger is usually pregnant for about three months. She will usually have two to four cubs. Some tigers have as many as seven cubs at once.

Cubs stay with their mother for up to two years.

FACT FILE

NAME:	Cub
NUMBER:	Usually two to four
PREGNANCY LENGTH:	Around three months
WHEN FULLY GROWN:	Three years

Cubs use the white spots on their mother's ears to follow her. When mothers sense danger, they flatten their ears, telling the cubs to hide.

Cats in Danger

Scientists list tigers as endangered. This means they are at risk of dying out. Tiger habitats have been damaged by human activity, such as building roads and cutting down forests.

Some people hunt tigers for their body parts and fur. Tiger body parts are used in certain types of medicine. Fortunately, other people are trying to stop the illegal selling of tiger body parts.

Some people are protecting habitats to keep tigers safe.

Cat Files

Tigers are incredible big cats. We have seen how good they are at blending into their habitats. Would you like to see a tiger in the wild?

Roar-Some Roundup

CONTINENT:	Asia
HABITAT:	Rainforests, savannas, mangrove swamps, and pine forests
FUR LENGTH:	Short
SIZE:	Up to 11 feet (3.5 m) long (without tail)
FOOD EATEN:	Up to 88 pounds (40 kg) in one night

How could you help protect tigers?

Glossary

agile able to move quickly and easily

camouflage to hide by blending into the surroundings

coastal describing areas of land near the sea

illegal not allowed by the law

mammal an animal that is warm-blooded, has a backbone, and makes milk to feed its young

pregnant when a female animal has one or more babies growing inside her

prey animals that are hunted by other animals for food

retractable able to be pulled back or in, such as claws

territory an area claimed and defended by an animal

Index